Sustainism is the New Modernism

Michiel Schwarz, Joost Elffers

a sustainist manifesto

In the last century, our
world was shaped by mod-
ernist ideas and values.
From the design of our
cities to our life-styles,
from our homes to our
technologies and our
ideas of progress, most
of twentieth-century life
in one way or another
reflects a modernist
c u l t u r e.

Now, at the beginning of the twenty-first century, we can see a new era emerging, one that embraces more sustainable ways of living. New attitudes to both the manmade and the natural environment, new approaches to both local and global issues, are developing throughout our society and indeed all over the world. What is coming into being is nothing less than a change in cultural perspective, a new mindset, an international remaking. Moving beyond ideas of modernism and postmodernism, this shared outlook promises a networked, globalized, sustainable future. We have coined a word for this new cultural era:

SUSTAINISM

The world has entered the Sustainist age. We can see manifestations of Sustainism all around us if we care to recognize them. This Sustainist manifesto charts some of the emerging features and patterns of Sustainism. It provides pointers for a future we already inhabit.

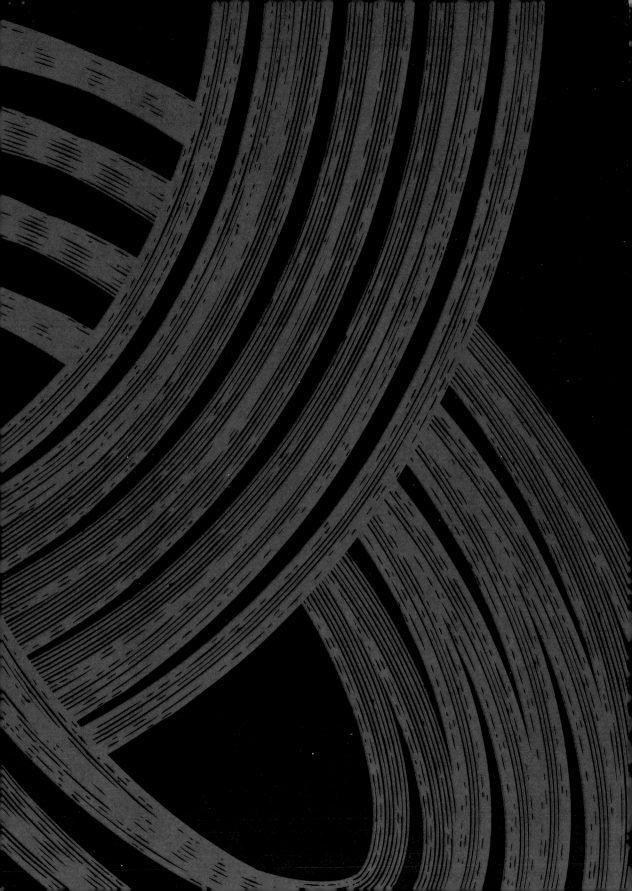

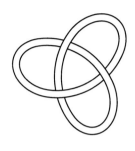

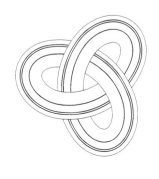

AFTER

MODERNISM

AND

POSTMODERNISM

COMES

SUSTAINISM

The trefoil knot is the symbol of sustainism.

sustainism

in

the

twenty-first

century

will

be

what

MODERNISM

WAS IN THE LAST

TO BRING N

INTO EX

WE FIRST

RENAME

EW CULTURE

ISTENCE

HAVE TO

THE WORLD

susta

inism

sus•tain•ism

\sə-stā-nìzzəm\ *noun.*

[from the Latin *sustinere*: to hold up, support, endure; and ismus: forming the name of a system of thought or practice [origins: derived from but going beyond sustainability and sustainable development, as it was used in the period around the end of the second millennium: relating to a life-style and society involving sustainable ways of living and practices, taking account of future generations, the natural environment, human needs and equity]
[first known use: c. 2009]

1 A worldwide twenty-first-century **cultural movement** and **cultural era**, in design, architecture, media, business, development, visual arts, life-styles, learning, technology, etc., characterized by ideas, practices, styles, methods, and expressions linked to concerns and values of sustainability, locality, interconnectedness., fairness, and a long-term view of human endeavor. It can be contrasted with the MODERNISM of the twentieth century (with which, however, it is also in some ways continuous): moving away from and beyond earlier industrialized, mechanistic, and rationalist approaches to the manmade environment, nature, business, design, and living, it is a movement oriented toward more sustainable and durable strategies for the future, acknowledging the power of networks. It embraces both low-tech and high-tech styles (often in combination) to find creative solutions to the world's issues both globally and in local contexts. As a social movement, it represents and conveys a direction (of looking, of seeing, of doing) but is not directive.

2 A way of looking, a collective **worldview** that stresses the interdependence among cultural and natural environments, local and global realities, and material and immaterial bases for sustainable human development, in a networked world.

3 A **paradigm** that defines and creates a culture of SUSTAINITY, as contrasted with and (in parts) linking to the culture of MODERNITY.

4 **Relating to** SUSTAINIST ideals, aesthetics, thoughts, values, systems of organization, and life-styles

sus•tai•nist

\sə- stā-nìst\ *noun* or *adjective*.

A noun.

1 A participant, sympathizer, or proponent of SUSTAINIST ways of living, values, or outlook.

2 An adherent or exponent of SUSTAINISM in any of field of culture, economy, or society; someone whose ideas, activities, work or life-style are characterized by SUSTAINISM (in various senses).

B *adjective.*

Of, relating to, or characteristic of SUSTAINISM or SUSTAINISTS (in various senses).

sus•tai•ni•ty

\sə- stā-nə-tē\ *noun.*

1 The contemporary era characterized by features of SUSTAINISM and by SUS-TAINIST ideas, practices, and styles.

2 The quality or condition of being SUSTAINIST in character or style.

3 Something that is SUSTAINIST; a SUSTAINIST example of something.

4 A condition that both transcends and extends MODERNITY, creating novel forms of living, expression, development, environment, etc., that encompass SUSTAINIST ideas and values.

a new word for a new world

CONTENTS

a new perspective:

a more connected attitude

to nature and our role in it,

a longer time perspective,

a new appreciation of place,

a changed view on what

we value and how

we make our world

THE AGE OF

SUSTAINISM

HAS BEGUN

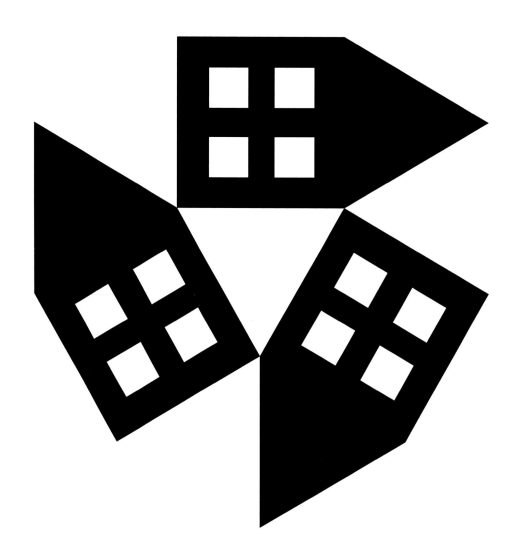

THE FUTURE OF OUR

BUILT ENVIRONMENT

AND OF OUR LIFE-WORLD

WILL BE SHAPED BY THE

IDEAS OF SUSTAINISM.

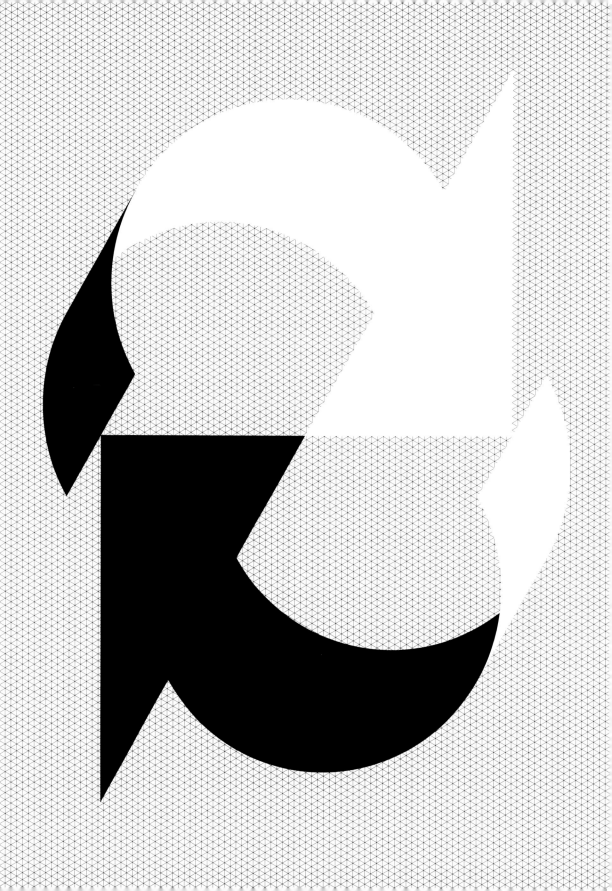

Sustainism is a cultural force.

Sustainism is a movement
without historical precedent:
worldwide but rooted in localism,
and with a cultural power that
needs no formal authority.

It represents
a shared set
of ideas and ideals,
an aesthetic style, a life-style.

Sustainism is
a way of seeing,
a way of being,
an attitude,
an emerging paradigm

Sustainism,
unlike modernism,
builds on a mass of engaged
people organized in millions of citizen-led organizations,
"the largest movement in the world."*

*Paul Hawken, *Blessed Unrest: How the Largest Movement in the World Came
into Being and Why No One Saw it Coming*, 2007. Hawken is describing
the 2 million or so nonprofit organizations around the world.

SUSTAINISM MARKS
THE ZEITGEIST AT
THE BEGINNING OF
THE TWENTY-FIRST
CENTURY:

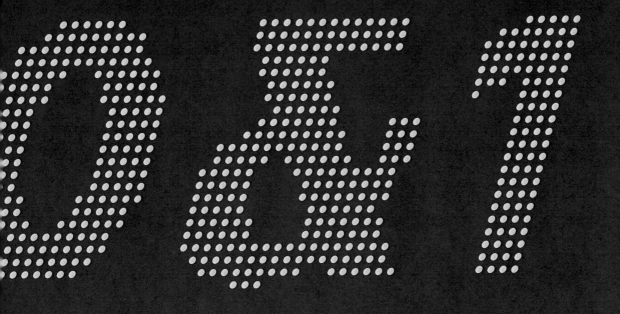

THE CONFLUENCE OF
GLOBALIZATION,
THE WEB,
CLIMATE CHANGE,
LOCALISM,
MEDIA DEMOCRACY,
OPEN SOURCE,
ENVIRONMENTALISM,
AND MORE.

a culture of sustainism

Culture as something we live in.
With a coherent worldview and
with its own set of ideas, symbols, values, and expressions.

And culture as something we have:
sustainist artifacts
sustainist media
sustainist architecture
sustainist design
sustainist art.

The Sustainability Revolution is in essence a revolution of culture

modernity

post

SUSTA

modernity

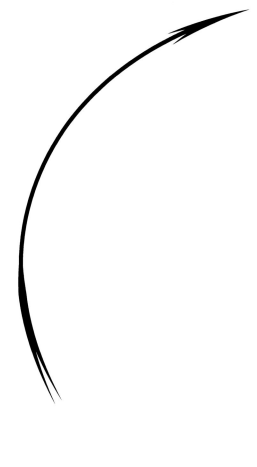

The transition
from a modernist to
a sustainist culture
affects everything:
how we make our world,
how we relate to nature,
what we see as possible,
desirable, and acceptable.

LOCAL & GLOBALIZED

ECOLOGICAL & DIGITAL

Manifestations of Sustainism are emerging in all of culture:
from architecture and design to how we deal with food and
our land, from media expressions and community
to innovation and urban life.

sustainist

networked

digital

localist

Sustainism
marks a shift not
only in thinking and doing
but in collective perception—
of how we live, do business, feed
ourselves, design, travel, and
communicate, as much as of
how we deal with nature
and development, and
of our roles in
them.

SUSTAINISM REPRESENTS A NEW CULTURAL ERA

sustainism has emerged around the ideas of environmental and social sustainability, durability, equity, and the open exchange of information.

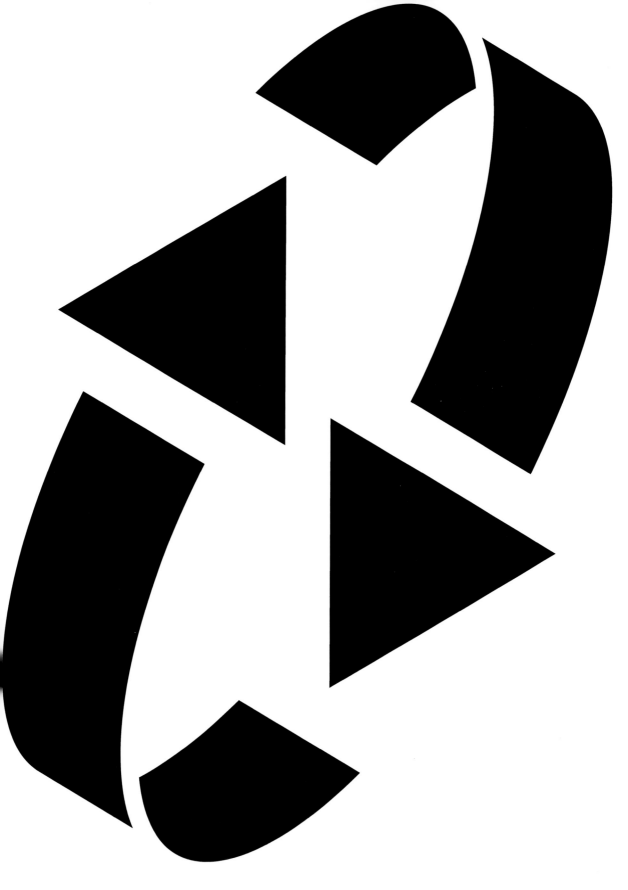

sustainist life =

sustainable x localist x

digital x global x

communityminded x

transparent x equitable x

handmade x hightech

x recyclable x diverse

The ethics of Sustainism are built on ideas of groundedness and stewardship: "Mother Earth" and "Spaceship Earth."*

* Kenneth Boulding, *The Economics of the Coming Spaceship Earth*, 1966, R. Buckminster Fuller, *Operating Manual for Spaceship Earth*, 1969.

Sustainism is adaptive, sensitive to changing contexts, and always evolving.

Sustainity is emerging as the new "mode of vital experience"* of twenty-first-century life.

*Marshall Berman, *All That Is Solid Melts into Air*, 1983.

To the younger generation it is obvious that the time of Sustainism is now—and they're embracing it (even though it hasn't been named as such).

As an ongoing project, Sustainism is never complete; it is open-ended and always in progress.

the nature of sustainity

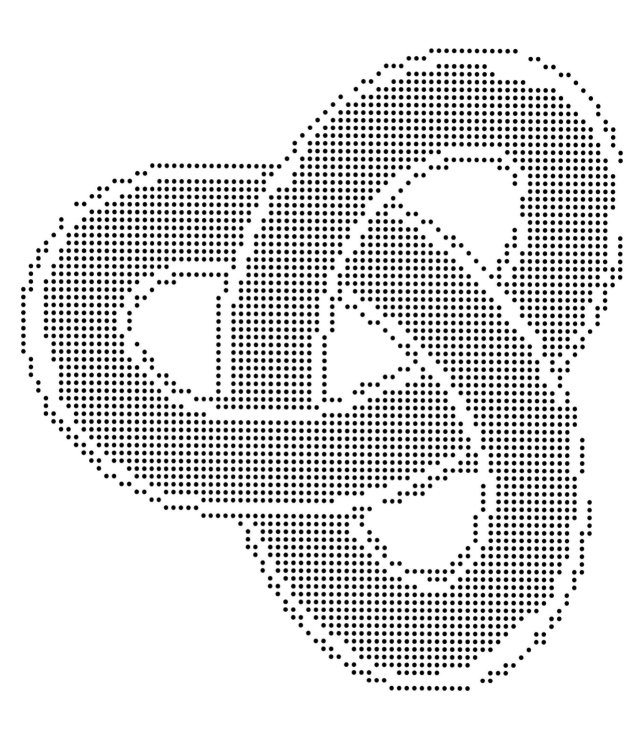

IN SUSTAINITY

EVERYTHING IS SEEN

AS INTERCONNECTED

AND INTERDEPENDENT,

A LIVING WEB

LOCAL X GLOBAL

SOLAR
POWER

"GLOCAL"

It sees crossovers and in-between spaces
as significant qualities.

But sustainity acknowledges the natural tensions
between local and global realities.

The interconnectedness of global issues becomes
apparent; "We cannot successfully address any of our
problems without addressing them all."*

*Barack Obama, Presidential weekly address, February 21, 2009.

Sustainity is not intent on making everything global but recognizes that all locals are globally connected

WIND
POWER

It is concerned with
proportionality
rather than scale

Both cultural diversity and biological diversity are essential qualities of sustainity

CRADLE-TO-CRADLE

in sustainist world-making there is :

no ecology without community

no development without equity

no design that is not codesigned

no value without shared meanings

no information that is not based on open source

no action without local consideration

no community without participation

no sustainability without fairness

SUSTA
PROC
A
CYC
RECU
REUJ
RECY

INIST

ESSES

RE

ICAL:

RRENT

SABLE

LABLE

sustainist
sense
is
the
new
common
sense

A lifestyle designed for permanence*

Social environments are as much part of our
ecology as the natural environment

Sustainist is not an individual property, but a property
of an entire network of relationships**

*E.F. Schumacher, *Small is Beautiful: Economics as if People Mattered*, 1973.

**Derived from Fritjof Capra, *The New Fact of Life:
Connecting the Dots on Food, Health, and the Environment*, 2009.

environmental
becomes
ecological
becomes
sustainable
creating a
culture of sustainity

FROM THE

MODERNIST

"MAKE IT NEW"

AND THE

POSTMODERNIST

"USE IT"

TO THE

SUSTAINIST

"REVITALIZE IT"

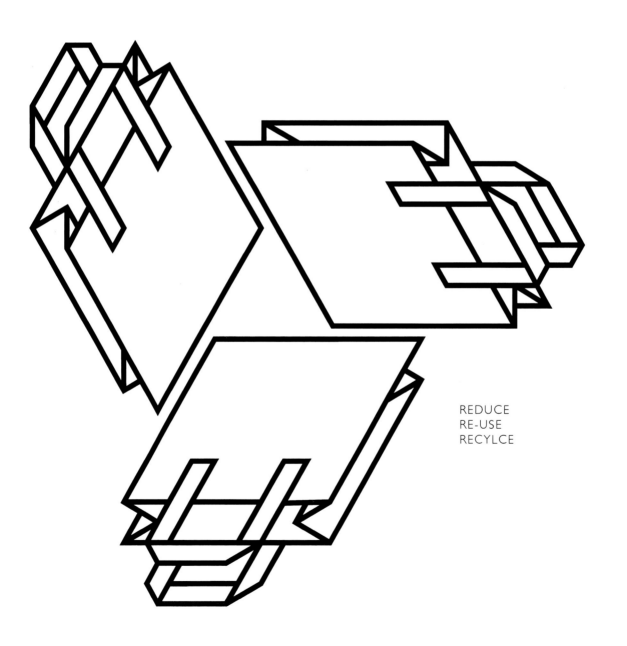

REDUCE
RE-USE
RECYLCE

sustainism versus modernism

Sustainism
favors diversity
over uniformity,
multiplicity over the singular.

sustainism rejects the universalism of modernity, not in the postmodern sense of denial of ultimate universal principles, but by looking for context as a measure of limits and appropriateness.

Sustainism embraces cyclical modes rather than the linearity of modernism; flow rather than structure

If modernity favored the square and the grid, sustainity tends to the round.

Where modernism shaped the environment of the "machine age," Sustainism defines the new ecology of the digital age.

"do more with less"

is the sustainist addition to modernism's minimalist "less is more."

*The first credo is attributed to R. Buckminster Fuller; the second to Ludwig Mies van der Rohe.

after

the hierarchical

world of modernism,

& the fragmented world

of postmodernism comes,

the networked

world of sustainism.

Where modernity
emphasized the material world,
sustainity incorporates the immaterial,
both in the physical and the philosophical sense.

If modernity
imagined the limitless,
sustainity sees the
creative power
of limits.

Sustainism
does not follow
the modernist pursuit of control over nature,
looking rather for ways
to work with nature.

Sustainism looks for what can be sustained,
rather than "the perishable, transitory, and the expendable"*
(as celebrated, for example, by the Futurists).

* Filippo Tomasso Marinetti, 1909.

sustainism

is the new

modernism*

* Michiel Schwarz, Joost Elffers, 2009.

Sustainism brings new senses of time,
as both more experiential and more durable.

Its temporal perspective

incorporates future generations :

The Clock of the Long Now *

* Stewart Brand, *Clock Of The Long Now: Time And Responsibility*, 2000.

Sustainism (re-)connects
the present to history
and the future to the present.

SEASONAL

local tempo

selective slowness

appropriate speeds

We are no longer blinded by the Futurist fascination
with "The Beauty of Speed."*

*Filippo Tommaso Marinetti, "Manifesto of Futurism," 1909

sustainism has a deep sense of place, grounded in local experience rather than global environments.

Sustainism
changes our
perspective on location:
geography shifts
from space
to place.

Moving beyond
the space age idea of
the world as one "global village,"*
Sustainism recognizes
that we now live in a
globe of villages.

*Marshall McLuhan, *The Gutenberg Galaxy*, 1962, and susbsequent books.

DO
MORE
WITH LESS

SUSTAINIST DESIGN IS

DESIGN WITH.

IT IS DESIGN WITH

PEOPLE RATHER THAN

DESIGN BESTOWED

ON PEOPLE; WITH

NATURE INSTEAD OF

COUNTERING NATURE

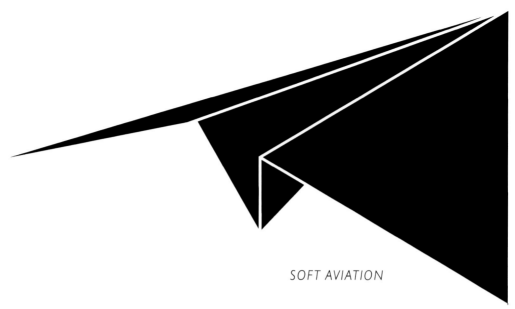

SOFT AVIATION

Sustainist design
connects with our
life-world, focusing not
just on function and form but
on the meanings we create
and the experiences
we produce.

The meaning
of a design is more
than its function and
its form: the modernist
credo "Form follows
function" is not
enough.

It adds
meaning to functionality
as a design principle

"Eventually everything connects. . . .
The quality of the connections are the key to quality."*

*Ray and Charles Eames [Sustainists avant la lettre], Power of Ten, 1977.

sustainist design

is responsible design;

it is socially and

environmentally

conscious

Modernism
could not deal
with complex systems*;
Sustainism lives with them.

*Tim Brown, IDEO, 2010.

*HYBRID
TRANSPORTATION*

Sustainism favors simplicity*, not to reduce things to their
simplest form but to incorporate the complexities of life—
including time, context, meaning, perpetual learning,
emotion, and trust.

*Based on John Maeda, *Laws of Simplicity*, 2006.

FUSIONS BETWEEN ECODESIGN AND HIGHTECH BECOME COMMONPLACE

In Sustainism's new styles, environment and technology are no longer in opposition.

Modernist Style

Less is more

Uniformity

Autonomous

Nature as resource

Planning

Form follows function

Machinelike

Linear

Structure

Minimalist

Reductionist

Objects

Centralized

Appropriation

Efficiency

Disposable

Do more with less

Diversity

Interdependent

Nature as source

Codesign

Meanings follow connections

Mirroring nature

Cyclical

SUSTAINIST Style

Flow

Variegated

Complex simplicity

Connections

Networked

Open-source exchange

Effectiveness

Recyclable

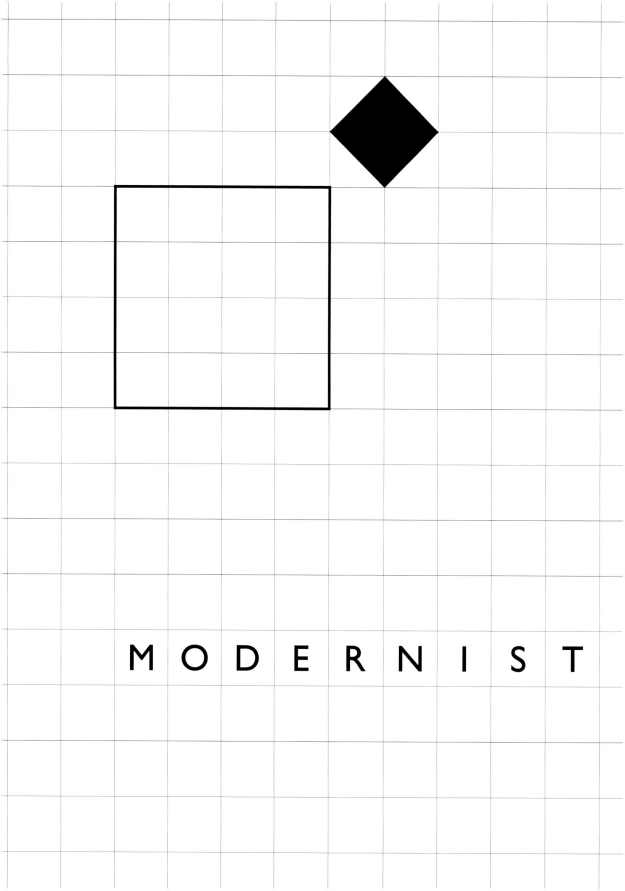

MODERNIST

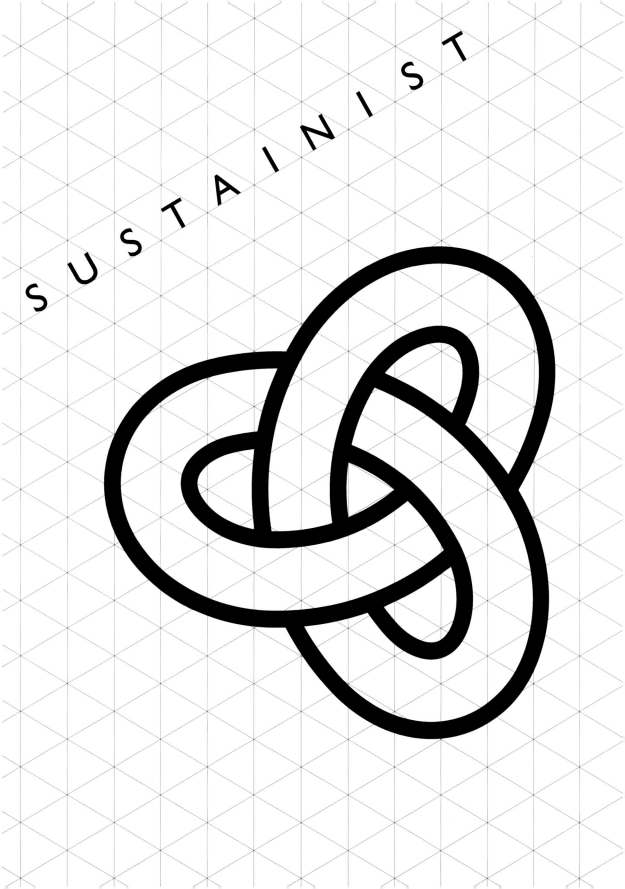

SUSTAINIST

sustainist media

From
"the medium is the message"*
to
"the media are the message.**

From
access to means of production
to
access to means of communication.

Internetworks
link
social networks,
sharing media
makes community.

*Marshall McLuhan, *Understanding Media: The Extensions of Man*, 1964.

**Joel ben Izzy, in conversation, Berkeley, 2010.

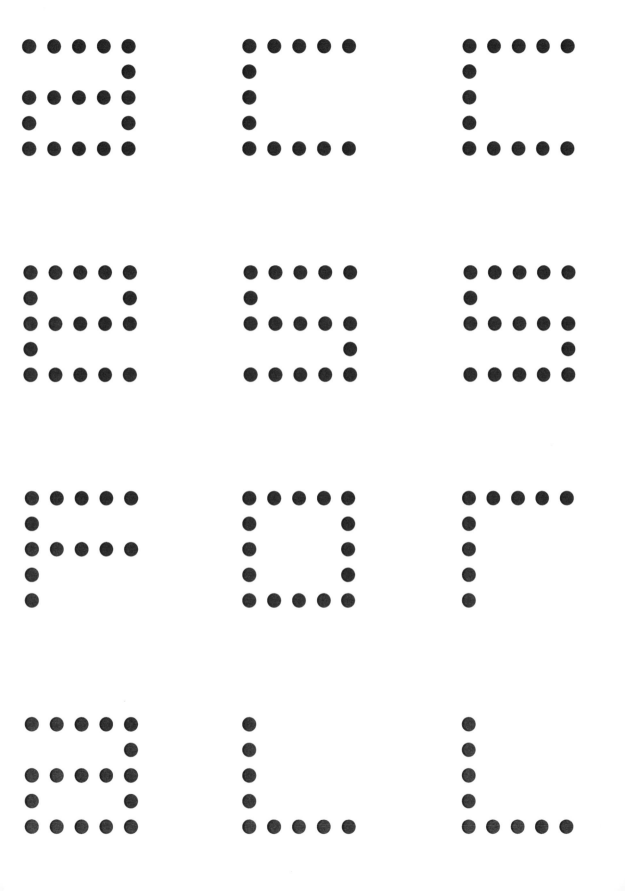

The Internet, as a social technology, is Sustainist by nature: based on sharing experiences, recycling and remixing information, linking people & communities, the local & the global, users & producers.

Social networks as
meeting places
in the growing
mediascape.

THE INTERNET

The
use of
cell phones
grows organically,
even in the poorest
countries of the world.

RE-MIX CULTURE*

*Lawrence Lessig, *Remix Culture: Making Art and Commerce in the Hybrid Economy*, 2008

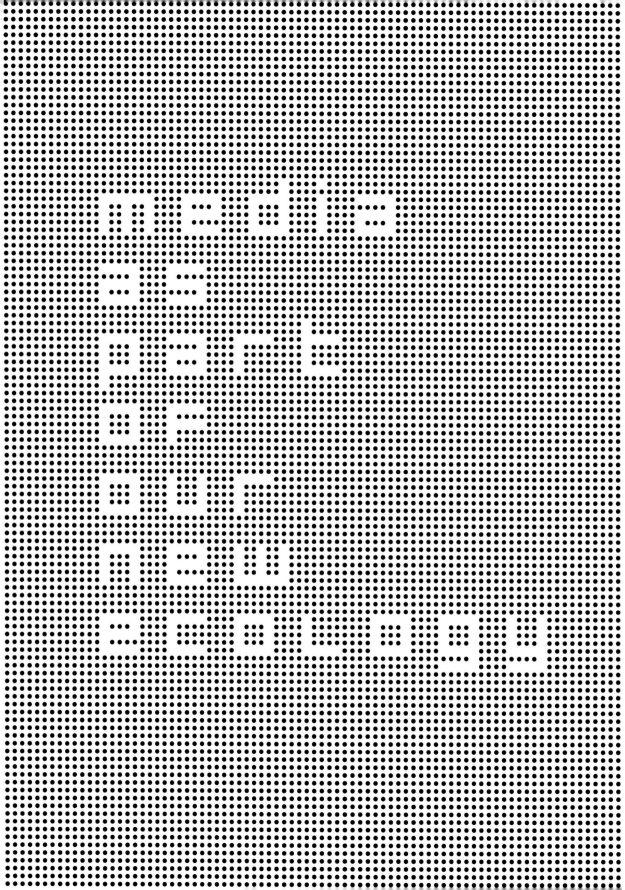

media
as
über
mem
üü
üeology

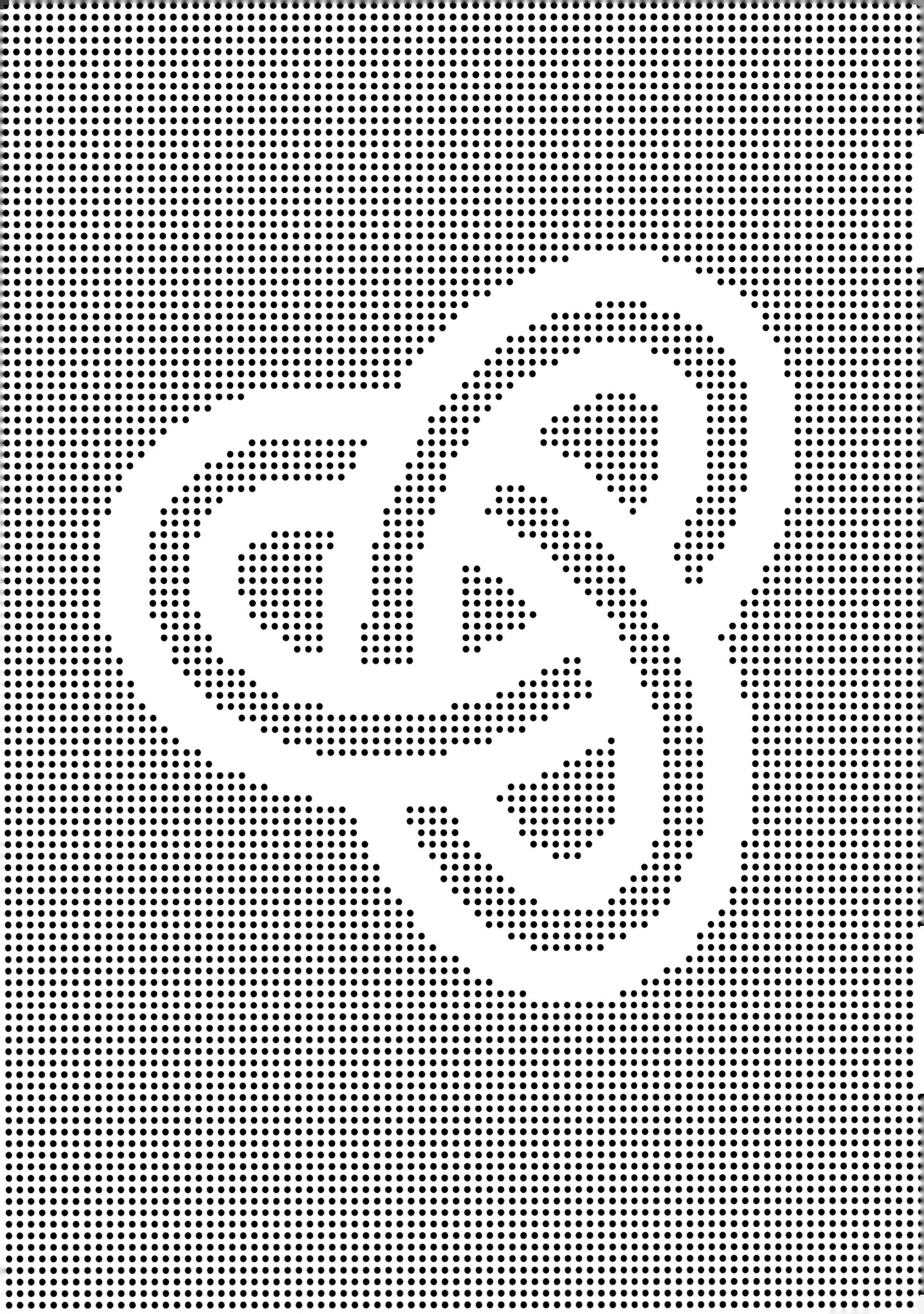

sustainist technologies

Not high-tech versus low-tech,
but appropriateness and sustainable solutions.

Home-grown technologies;
users design and shared apps.

Technologies acknowledged as social designs.

FROM TECHNOLOGIES

THAT IMPOSE ON CULTURE

TO A SUSTAINIST

TECHNO-CULTURE

SUSTAINIST

HIGH-TECH

QUALITIES

LIGHT

VERSATILE

LOW - ENERGY

MINIMAL-RESOURCE

INTERACTIVE

OPEN

SHARED

RECYCABLE

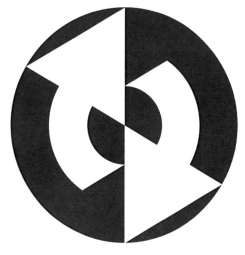

SUSTAINIST ARCHITECTURES ARE NOT LIMITED TO "GREEN" ARCHITECTURE BUT INCLUDE IT

They are
architectures
of connection
interface
intersection
crossover

Connecting
the architecture
of materiality
to the architecture of flows and networks

Just like your computer is your
personal and shared information vehicle,
your building becomes your power plant.*

In both physical space and cyberspace,

sustainist architectures move

from linear to nonlinear solutions,

from formal to informal environments,

from rigid hierarchies to dynamic interactions.

*Based on a statement by Jeremy Rifkin at the European Commission's
Research Connection meeting, Prague, 7 May 2009

CREATING INTERPLAYS BETWEEN "DATATECTURE" & PHYSICAL ARCHITECTURE

ORGANIC EGGS

Sustainist architectures are globalist in their sustainable technologies, localist in their qualities.

"Situation design" is as relevant as infrastructural design.

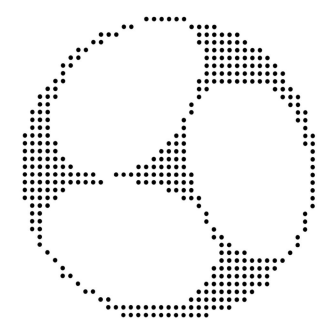

THE

CULTURE

OF

SUSTAINITY

WILL

TRANSFORM

ART

ART
WILL
TRANSFORM
THE
CULTURE
OF
SUSTAINITY

sustainist local

LOCAL

Sustainist logo:
LOCAL
A new label indicating local production and/or local produce.
Can be used to indicate a region or state or a specified
maximum travel distance.

NATIONAL TRADE

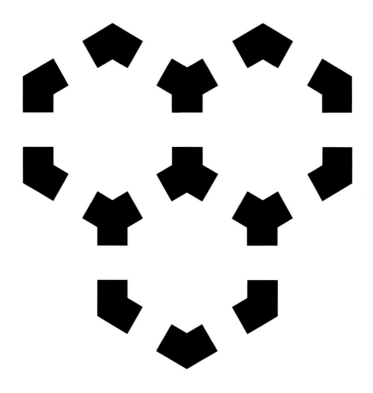

LOCAL TRADE

GLOBAL TRADE

LOCAL

IS A QUA

NOT

A CHOCR

MARKER

LITY

Localism = community + sustainable life-style.

APHICAL

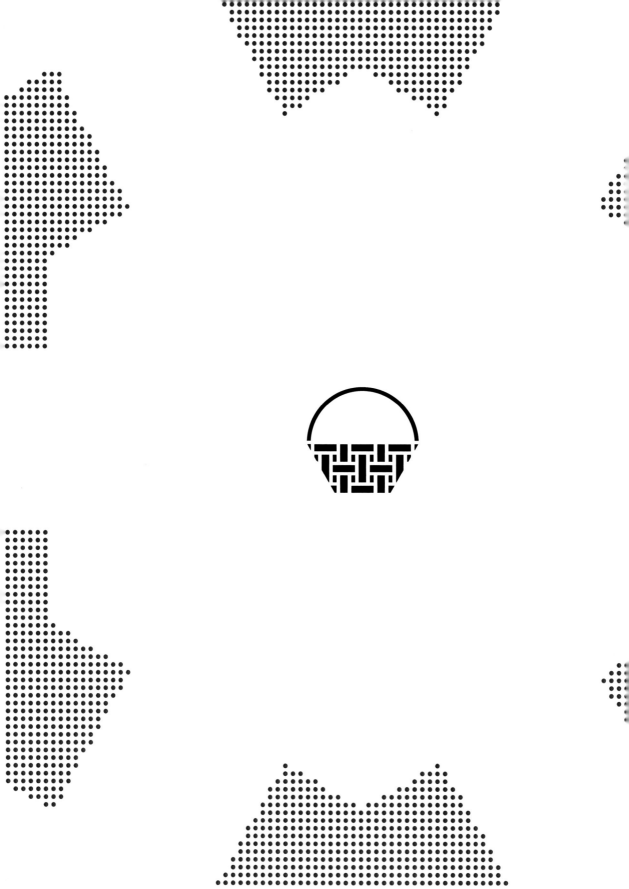

Local as an ethical ,
aesthetic, and cultural
Q U A L I T Y ,
shared in a community .

Sustainist Hexagon: The Open Citadel
Form: citadel; honeycomb.
Sustainist Symbol: local; place and community in a globalized world.

FARMERS

MARKET

the conceptual model

of local culture

local economy

and local

community

Local markets do more than sell local produce;
they are meeting places, where we meet
the producers and connect with the source.

New forms of localism become the basis for economies.

Localism opens up opportunities
for new forms of neighborhood.

sustainist habitats

SEASONAL

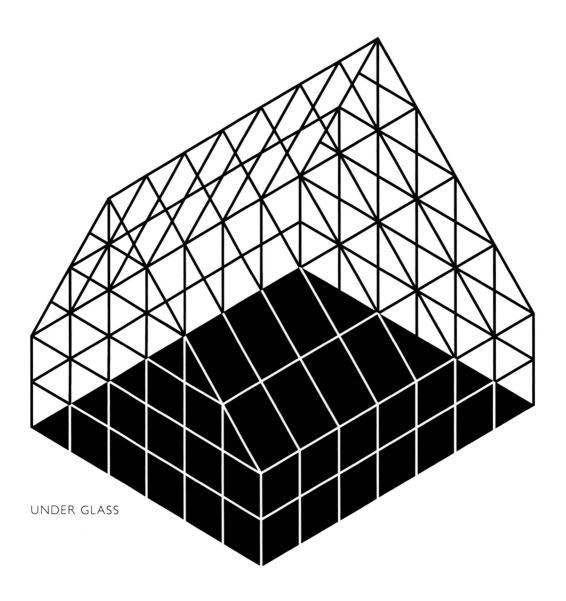

UNDER GLASS

sustainism acknowledges that global warming changes much more than the climate: it transforms the way we look at our habitats and how we inhabitat them

Inhabiting a sustainist life-style implies
lowering energy use and reducing carbon impacts.

To sustain our global habitat, the energy base shifts from
carbon-based to renewable fuels, turning "from fuels from hell
to fuels from heaven."*

*Thomas L. Friedman, *Hot, Flat, and Crowded*, 2008

From energy supplied by a distant anonymous producer,
to something you create yourself and share
with your neighbours.

Inspired by Bill McKibben,
Deep Economy: The Wealth of Communities and the Durable Future, 2007.

A HABITAT

OF MUTUAL

RELATIONSHIPS

FROM YOU ARE

WHAT YOU HAVE

TO YOU ARE

WHAT YOU SHARE

NATURE

AS A SOURCE

RATHER THAN

AS A RESOURCE

Human
life is mirrored
in nature; nature
is mirrored in
human life.

Nature
is understood as
neverending—it's our
changing ideas of
nature that come
and go.

Culture/nature:
urban farming as a
new sustainist form.

principals of biomimicry*

nature:

recycles

rewards cooperation

banks on diversity

demands local expertise

runs on sunlight

uses only the energy it needs

fits form to function

taps the power of limits

curbs excesses from within

*as formulated by *Janine M. Benyus in Biomimicry: Innovation Inspired by Nature,* 1997

the nature of sustainity

a sustainist culture:

recycles
rewards cooperation
banks on diversity
demands local expertise
runs on renewable energy
uses only the energy it needs
relates form to meanings
taps the power of limits
sustainist sense of proportionality

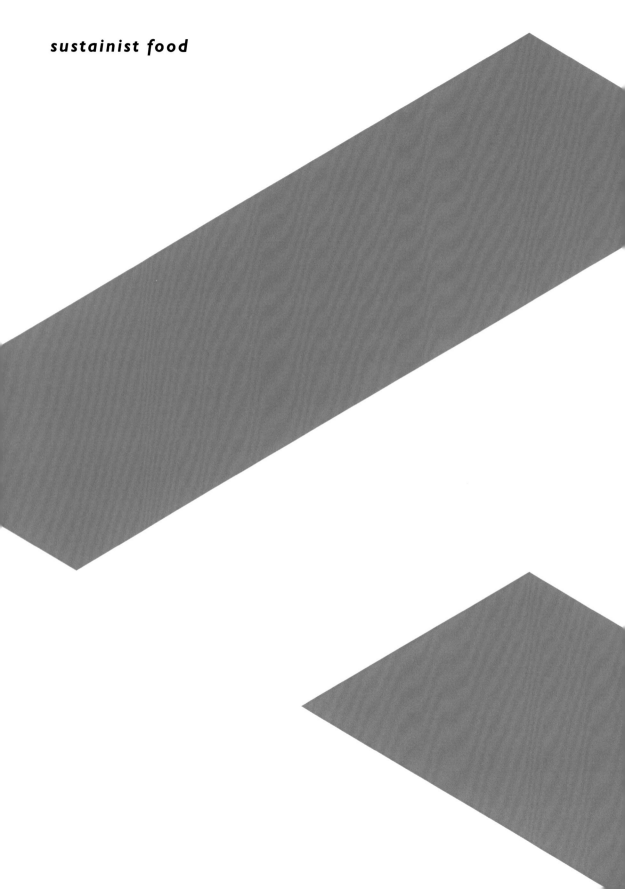

sustainist food

in

valuing

time

and

place

we value

seasonal

and

local

foods.

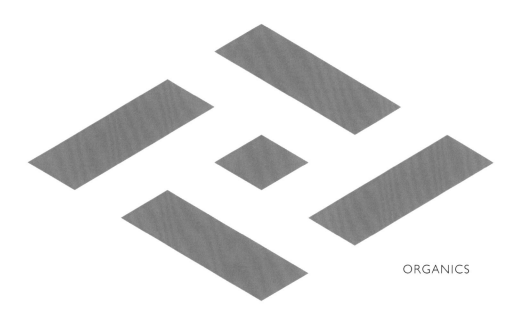

ORGANICS

from food as a global
economic commodity
to food as part of local
experience and community.

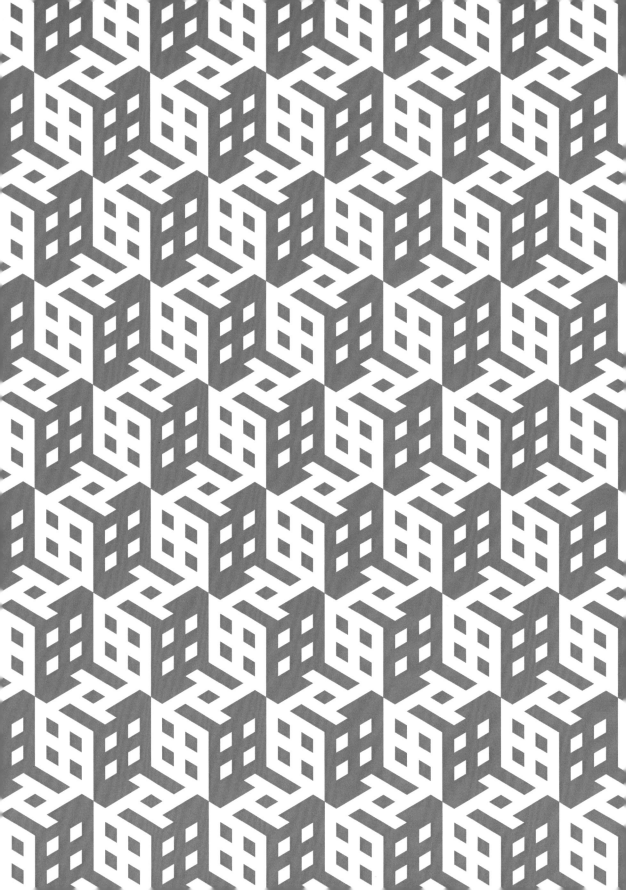

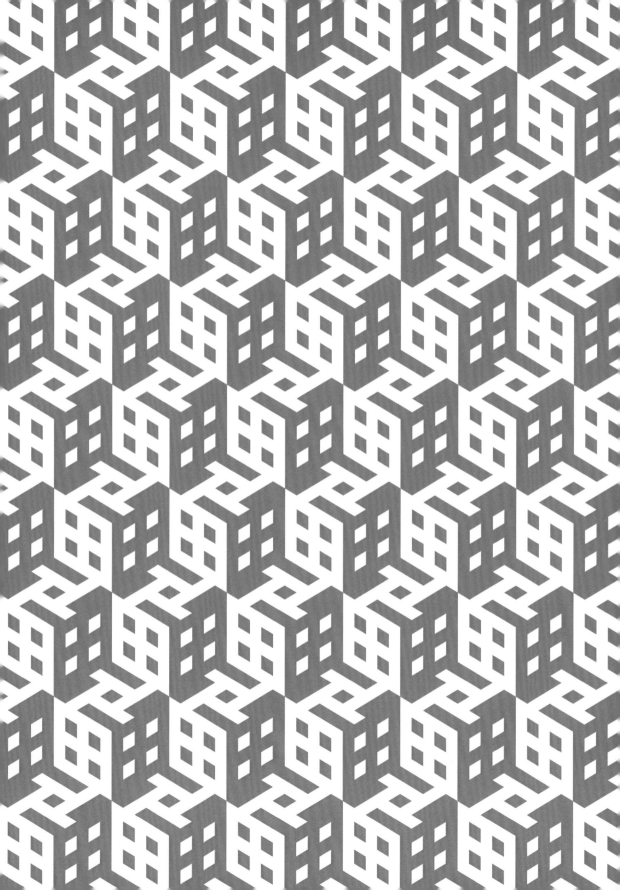

eating as an agri-cultural act*

*Wendell Berry, *What Are People For?*, 1990.

A new "food culture" is growing.

From global food to locally grown:
we are becoming "locavores."

Transition Culture*: Re-instating the idea that food
is something that grows near where you live,
by someone you have some kind of a relationship with,
and that you actually cook yourself.

Transition Culture, Tamzin Pinkerton and Rob Hopkins,
Local Food: How to Make it Happen in Your Community, 2009.

"Edible Schoolyard"* as an inspirational model:
urban garden, kitchen, classroom—food as a single project.

*The original Edible Schoolyard program was initiated by the Chez Panisse
Foundation and Alice Waters in Berkeley, California, in 1995.

ROOFTOP
ORGANICS

BACKYARD
ORGANICS

Everything is connected:
the entire food chain is reflected
in what we eat, running from
the soil to the plate.

Beyond the modernist
concept of nutritionism.

Food as total nourishment
for the body, the senses,
the mind, and the earth.

Sharing food = creating community.

The food on our plate is our most important engagement with the natural world, and the biggest impact we have on climate change* as well as on our health.

*Taken from an interview with Michael Pollan.

sustainist learning & innovation

Play-as-learning never stops; in the true spirit of "education permanente," it is endlessly recyclable.

"Cultural Creatives"* as drivers of the movement towards Sustainism

Man as SYMBOL-MAKER as well as TOOL-MAKER** — bringing the culture of art and the culture of technology together again.

Sustainist innovation is less competitive and exclusive and more collaborative and inclusive.

**Lewis Mumford, *Art & Technics*, 1951,

*Paul H. Ray and Sherry Ruth Anderson, *The Cultural Creatives: How 50 Million People Are Changing the World*, 2000

LEARNING

TO CONNECT

Community
of practice
at the heart
of creativity
and learning.

IN ALL

KINDS OF WAYS

The "Creative Commons"* sets the norm for questions of "copyright" and "copyleft": to have a choice whether what we know and what we create may be kept, shared and freely used, or should be protected and paid for.

*Creative Commons: http://creativecommons.org/.

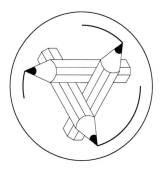

Sustainism encourages free culture* an unrestricted exchange of ideas and information.

*Lawrence Lessig, *Free Culture: How Big Media Uses Technology and the Law to Lock Down Culture and Control Creativity*, 2004.

A new ethic
of dialogue : a
flow of shared
meanings.
(from the Greek
dia-logos):

OPEN SOURCE
IS THE MODE
AND METAPHOR
FOR CREATIVE
INNOVATION

Sustainism values
individual quality and
excellence within a
spirit of sharing
and collaboration.

Sustainism embraces "We-Think"*—innovation
through collaborative and bottom-up "mass creativity."
(Wikipedia and Linux are exemplars.)
*Charles Leadbeater, *We-Think*, 2008.

Social innovation
is spurred by
combining
bottom-up
top-down, and
horizontal
approaches
incorporating
social networks
new technologies
& strategic
coalitions*

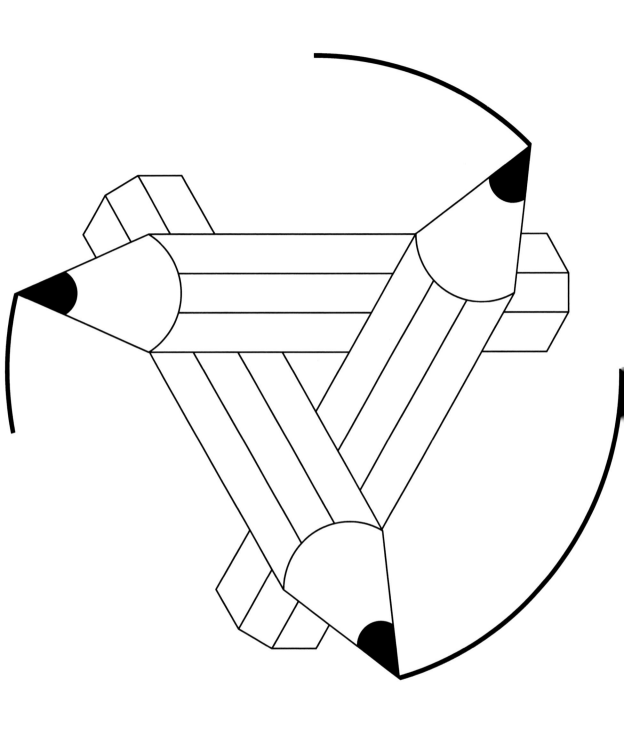

*Inspired by Geoff Mulgan and The Young Institute, London.

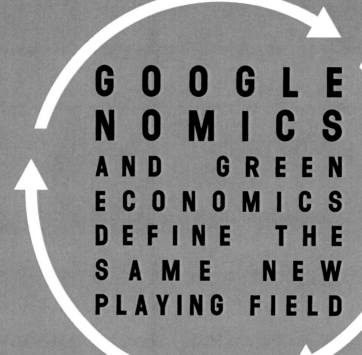

GOOGLE
NOMICS
AND GREEN
ECONOMICS
DEFINE THE
SAME NEW
PLAYING FIELD

Sustainist values
—sharing, cooperation, collaboration, openness—
create added value.

A selective Capitalism:
more concerned with society and ecology, and more
selective about what to grow and what not.*

*Geoff Mulgan, "After Capitalism", *Prospect*, April 2009

Social business* as sustainist model.

*Muhammad Yunus, *Building Social Business:*
The new kind of capitalism that serves humanity's most pressing needs, 2010.

Nature and environment are true costs
incorporated in our economic equations.

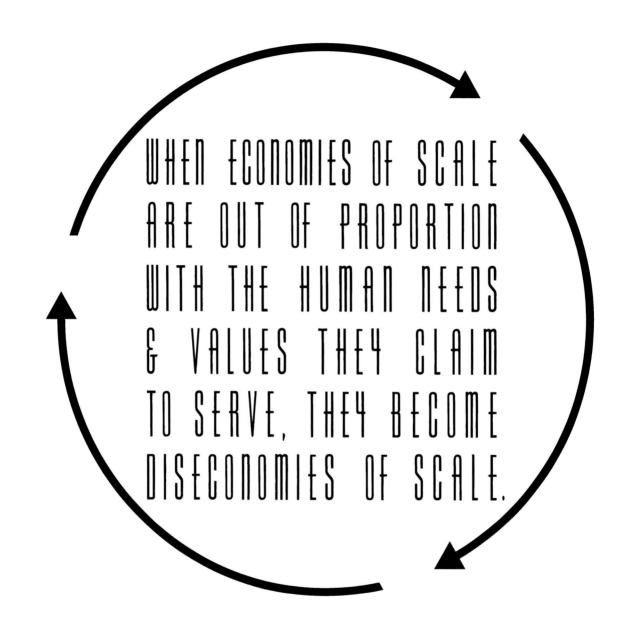

WHEN ECONOMIES OF SCALE
ARE OUT OF PROPORTION
WITH THE HUMAN NEEDS
& VALUES THEY CLAIM
TO SERVE, THEY BECOME
DISECONOMIES OF SCALE.

"Eco-equity"
—equality for all and protection for all—
as the basis for "green business"* models.

*Van Jones, *The Green Collar Economy:
How One Solution Can Fix Our Two Biggest Problems*, 2008.

The marketplace wants "less of more"*—
more diverse products in lower quantities rather
than fewer products in higher quantities.

*Chris Anderson,
The Long Tail: Why the Future of Business Is Selling Less of More, 2006.

The rise of "ethonomics"*
— an ethical economics, incorporating
sustainability, accountability, design and social
responsibility into business practices.

*The term was first proposed by *Fast Company*
(Noah Robischon) in February 2009

From a market of desires to a market of needs.

THE NEW ECONOMY BECOMES THE GREEN ECONOMY BECOMES THE SUSTAINIST ECONOMY

Sustainist CRADLE-TO-CRADLE logo.
This logo is designed to represent Cradle-to-Cradle as a mentality,
a state of mind. The triangular symbol refers to recycling, re-use, self-
sufficiency. It represents closed and dynamic cycles of material life
and energy. Here it denotes products, designs or systems that support
the idea of eco-effectiveness: waste = resource.

From eco-efficiency

to eco-effectiveness,

waste

becomes

resource,

"cradle-to-cradle." *

*William McDonough and Michael Braungart, *Cradle-to-Cradle: Remaking the Way We Make Things*, 2002.

Production can
be digital or physical—
whatever takes less energy
and minimizes resource use.

Smart consumerism equals socially and
environmentally conscious consumption.

Carbon footprints and ecological footprints
are indicators for sustainist production
and consumption.

Production and consumption
fueled by renewables.

FROM LINEAR TO CYCLICAL MODES

IN HOW WE MAKE & USE THINGS

TO RECYCLE

AND

REUSE

RATHER THAN

REPLACE

AND

THROW AWAY

LONGEVITY REPLACES REPLACEMENT

Carbon footprint: economy versus ecology.
Transporting this book (with thousands of other copies)
from China to the U.S. by sea freight and then by truck
to the bookstore produced an estimated
1500 kg of CO2 greenhouse gas (value is indicative).

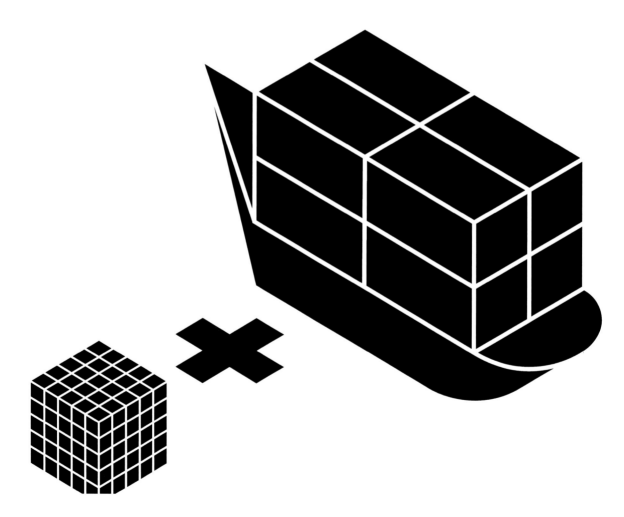

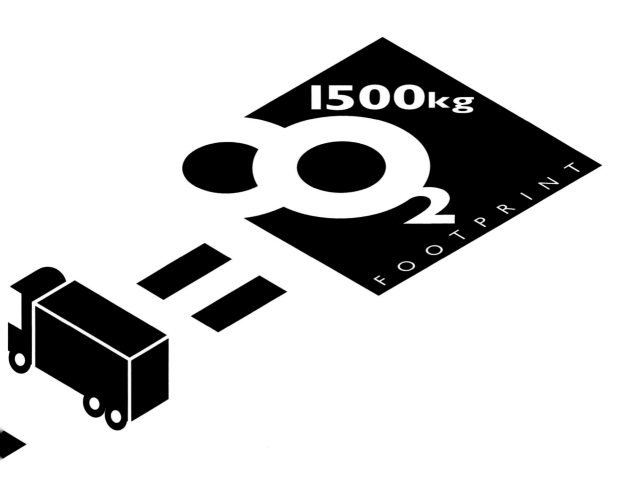

CO2 FOOTPRINT

1500kg

Had you been willing to pay 50% more for this book, it would have been printed in the U.S.A., resulting in a considerable reduction of its transport-related carbon footprint.

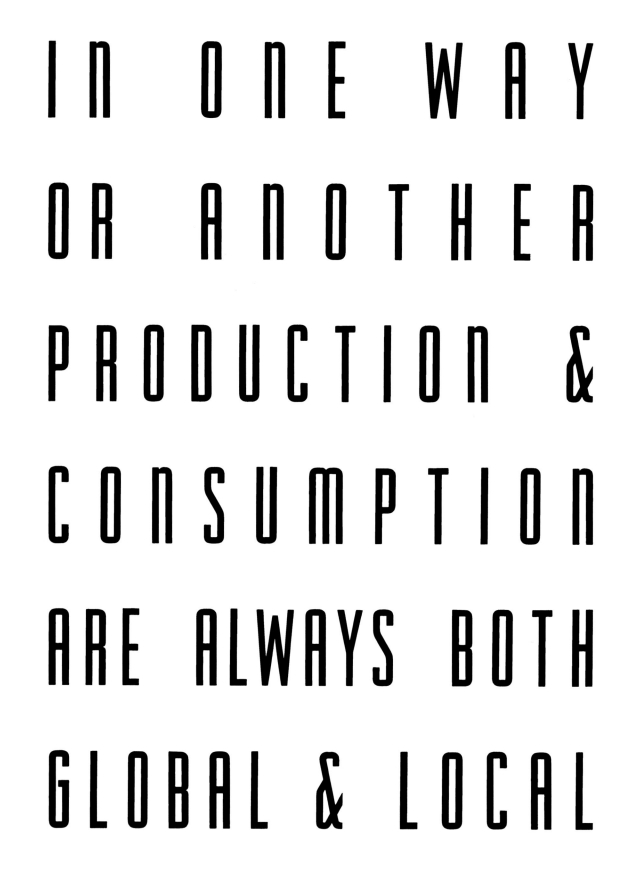

IN ONE WAY
OR ANOTHER
PRODUCTION &
CONSUMPTION
ARE ALWAYS BOTH
GLOBAL & LOCAL

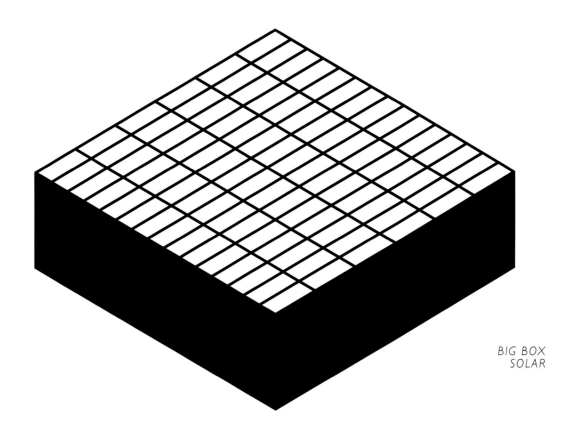

BIG BOX
SOLAR

MODES OF
PRODUCTION

RESPONSIBLE
FAIR
EFFECTIVE
LIGHT IMPACT

Sustainist logo:
CARBON FOOTPRINT
*design for a generic label to the CO_2 greenhouse
gas emissions of a given activity or product.*

A 100-mile car drive.
Producing a carbon footprint of 43 kg CO_2
added to the earth's atmposhere.
(based on an automobile running
on gasoline with 20 mpg).

Sustainist logo:
FOSSIL FUEL FOODPRINT (FFF)
*design for a new generic food label to compare impacts
of food production & transport in terms of fossil fuel use.
Indicates the ratio between food energy calories gained
and the fossil fuel equivalent to produce those food calories.*

Breakfast Cereal
FFF: Fossil Fuel Foodprint = 1:7
To produce 1 Food calorie needs
7 calories of Fossil Fuel energy.
Per serving of 100gr:
157 Food calories requires
1099 calories of Fossil Fuel energy input.

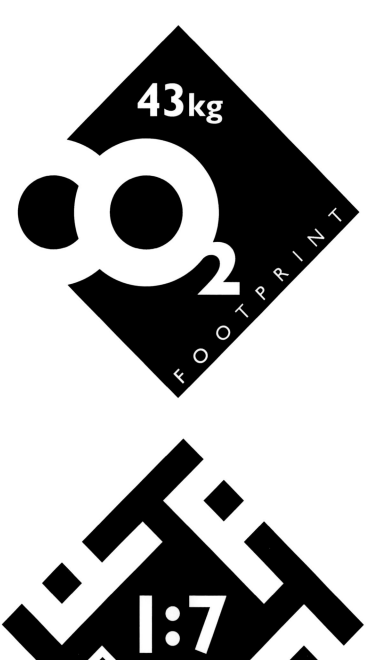

43kg

O₂ FOOTPRINT

1:7

FOSSIL FUEL FOODPRINT

Local and global knowledge are connected.

from

KNOWLEDGE

is

POWER

to

THE

POWER

OF

SHARED

KNOWLEDGE

GLOBAL

NETWORKS

as cultural agents

of knowledge for

ANYONE

ANYWHERE

ANYTIME

Individual quality
connects with
collective intelligence.

Knowledge for empowerment.

Re-instating the value of craftsmanship* as a Sustainist
quality, combining skill, commitment and judgment.

Richard Sennett, *The Craftsman, 2008*

we're all

becoming

our own experts

(with the internet

a major resource)

SPECIALIZATION IN
A SUSTAINIST ERA:

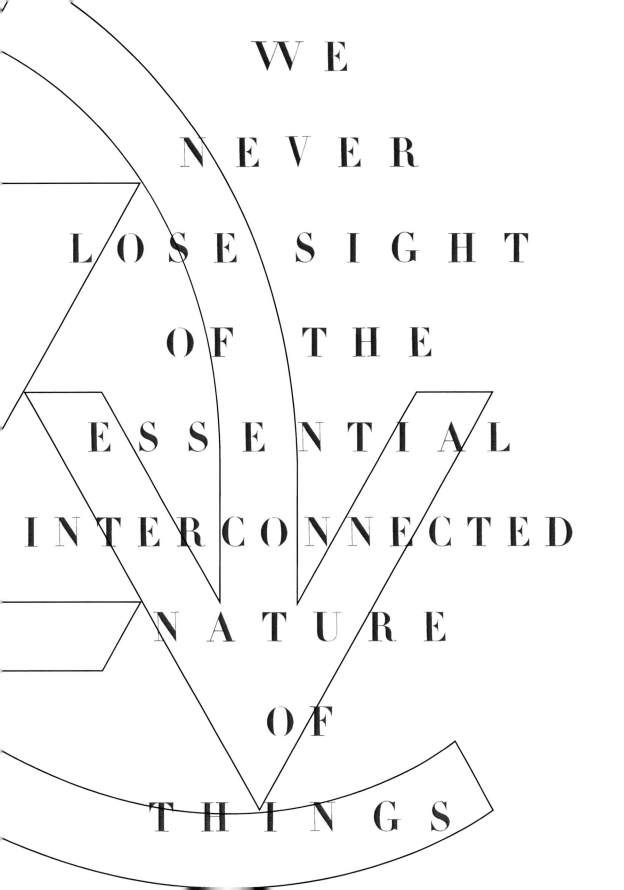

WE
NEVER
LOSE SIGHT
OF THE
ESSENTIAL
INTERCONNECTED
NATURE
OF
THINGS

Sustainism is not a religion, but can include it.

Compassion — the "golden rule" underpinning
most religious faiths — involves responsibility
for a sustainable future.

Many Heavens,
One Earth:
Faith Commitments
for a
Living Planet*

*The title of the 2009 "Celebration of Faiths and the Environment",
the first large-scale gathering by leaders of the world's major faiths — Baha'ism,
Buddhism, Christianity, Daoism, Hinduism, Islam, Judaism, Shintoism and Sikhism,
in Windsor Castle, UK, November 2-4, 2009

Forecast: A new great religion will arise
out of the environmental movement.*

*Forecaster Paul Saffo, KQED Radio, 31 December 2008.

sustainist christianity

A global agreement on climate change concerns equity, justice and the equal right to development. We are the stewards of God's creation. We need climate justice.*

*Keynote address by Rev. Dr Samuel Kobia,
General Secretary of the World Council of Churches,
a fellowship of 349 churches, representing 560 million Christians,
Lobby Dinner, Copenhagen, 13 December 2009.

THE
ENVIRONMENT
IS
GOD'S GIFT
TO
EVERYONE

(says Josef Ratzinger, Pope Benedict XVI) *
*Message of his Holiness Pope Benedict XVI
for the celebration of the World Day of Peace 2008

sustainist islam

A Muslim 7-year Action Plan:
"It is religious duty to safeguard our environment and to advocate the importance of preserving it."*

*Sheikh Ali Goma'a, grand mufti of Egypt on the announcement of a Muslim seven-year action plan on the environment, endorsed by Muslim scholars and environment ministries of many Muslim countries, 4 November 2009.

MOTHER
–
EARTH

(Prithvi Mata)*

*In the Hindi scriptures, the earth is addressed as Mother-Earth,
and personified as the goddess Bhumi. Our relationship to Mother-Earth
can be found in the Vedic "Hymn to the Earth" (Prithvi Sükta, in Atharva Veda,
1500 B.C.), which is probably the oldest "ecological" invocation.

sustainist hinduism

The essence of all religions is one.
Only their approaches are different.*

*Mahatma Gandhi.

All religions

are sustainist,

one way

or another.

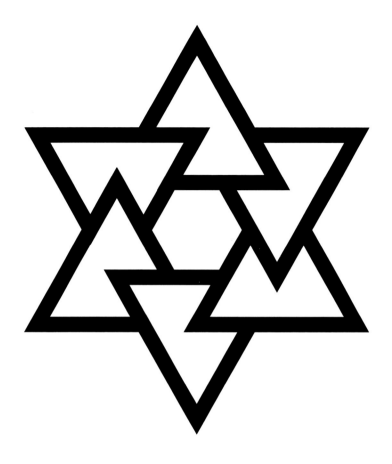

sustainist judaism

The vision for Judaism: "That the Jewish community
transform itself in relation to living healthily
and sustainably by September 2015, at the end
of the next shmita (sabbatical) year in Jewish time,
so to protect and conserving God's
creation in practical ways."*

*The Jewish Climate Change Campaign,
in 'Faith Commitments to Protect the Living Environment' Many Heavens,
One Earth, 3rd November 2009, Windsor Castle, UK

The world's

great religions

are embracing

sustainism.

sustainist buddhism

"We need to take corrective action to ensure a safe climate future for coming generations of human beings and other species. Buddhists, concerned people of the world and all people of good heart should be aware of this and act upon it."*

* The Fourteenth Dalai Lama, Endorsement, December 20, 2008, in A Buddhist Response to Climate Change, 2009.

sustainist health

From body culture to a culture of care.

The body as an organism in the ecology of life

Addressing the well-being of society implies
taking care of our personal health—
physical, mental, and spiritual.

From modern medicine to sustainist health.
From medical treatments to prevention
and life-style changes.

THE BODY IS NOT A
MACHINE THAT CAN
BE REGULATED &
PERFECTED BUT
AN ORGANISM IN
TUNE WITH ITS
ENVIRONMENT

healthy   soil
food
eating
movement
environment
materials
water
mind
body
air

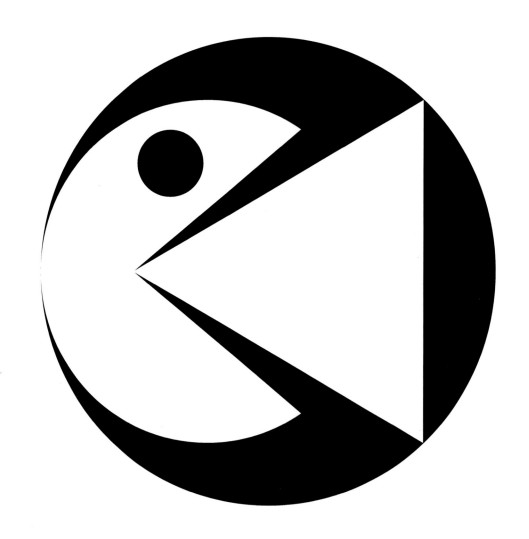

CHILD OBESITY

Neighborhood as an organizing principle,
literally and metaphorically.

AT THE

CENTER OF

COMMUNITY

IS CONNECTIVITY

Public governance is reimagined and redesigned
to emerge from local place, culture, and people.

Community is coherent, self-organized, and informal.

THE WEB AS A
METAPHOR FOR
COMMUNITY IN
THE SUSTAINIST ERA
DISTRIBUTED &
INTERCONNECTED
IN ANY SCALE

From technofix to social innovation.

Sustainist community politics as a "cultural politics."

The commons* as the sustainist model for democratic, equitable, and sustainable governance.

*See, for example Peter Barnes, *Capitalism 3.0: A guide to reclaiming the commons*, 2006.

OPEN SOURCE IS THE

CULTURAL

OPERATING SYSTEM *

THAT ELEVATES BOTH

THE INDIVIDUAL

AND

THE GROUP AT ONCE

*Kevin Kelly, in *Wired*, June 2009.

Sustainist Trefoil Knot:
The Sustainist Symbol
Form:
three-fold dynamic spatial unit; prime non-trivial knot
with three crossings; simplest 3-D closed cycle.
Sustainist Symbol:
interdependence; connecting nature and culture;
loops of life; recycleable; Sustainist living.

The three-dimensional trefoil symbolizes the closed loop
of sustainist life — endless, interdependent and cyclical. It is
based on a centuries old sign, reflecting the threefold forces
of nature (earth, air and water). The three-looped shape (the
simplest complex knot) of the Sustainist trefoil is founded
on the geometry of the triangle, a basic structural form in
architecture and design, as well as in nature.

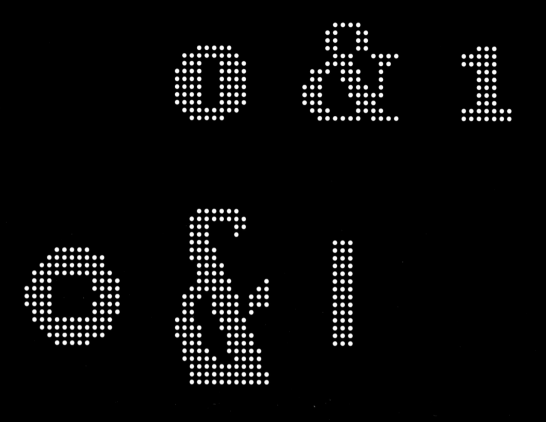

0 & 1
0 & 1
0 & 1

INCLUSIVENESS
IN A SUSTAINIST
DIGITAL WORLD

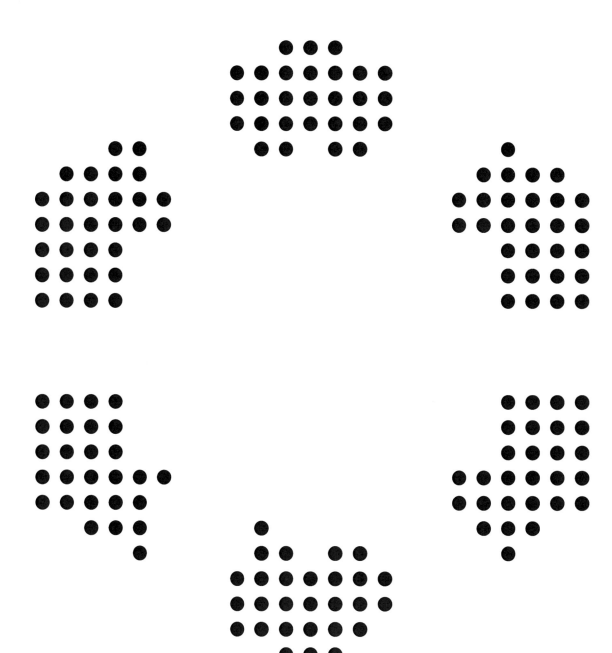

Sustainist Logo:
Open HEXAGON

The symbol for LOCAL is based on a hexagon, mirroring the citadel and the fortified cities of history, as well as the beehive honeycomb shapes that are found in nature We have designed the open hexagon. Opening it symbolizes the sustainist qualities of inclusiveness and open culture. In the connected world of sustainity, the 'local" will be recast.

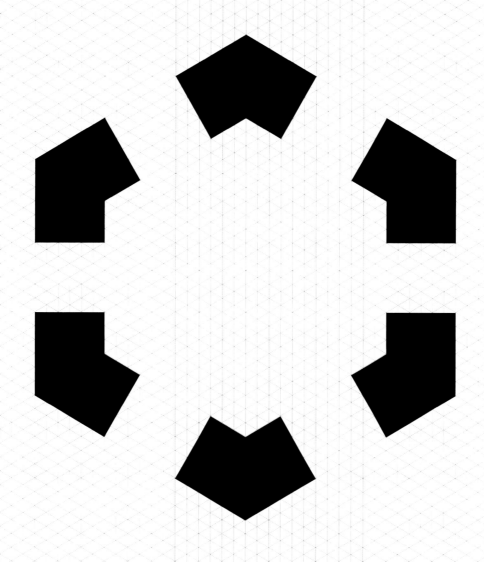

Sustainist Logo:
LOCAL

The design of the sustainist symbol for "local" is the open hexagon.
More than a geographic reference it denotes place, local qualities
and community. In sustainity the importance to communicate
"local" will grow —in production, market produce, and place-based
identity.

Cities are
living organisms
with their own natural
and social ecology.

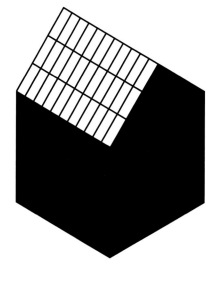

New strategies for
megacities in response
to climate change,
"models to sustain our
way of life" in an increas-
ingly urbanized world".*

Cities as sustainist hubs,
meeting places where
things and people connect.

Creating a new kind of metropolis
("mother city") integrating sustainist energy
flows, sustainist transport lines, sustainist
buildings, and sustainist infrastructures.

*Bill Clinton, Clinton Climate Initiative, 2009.
**Manuel Castells, *The Information Age (trilogy)*, 1996, 1997, 1998.

URBAN LIFE SEEN AS A SPACE OF FLOWS:** PEOPLE, INFORMATION, & NETWORKS, PHYSICAL, & DIGITAL.

finding local

identities

in a global

world beyond

the globalization

of the local

Cities
as sustainist hubs,
meeting places where
things and people connect,
with one another and
with other worlds.

The politics of
urban place are based on
autonomy but acknowledge
the interconnectedness
of economies, people,
information, and
energy.

Creating
new forms of
"ecological democracy,"*
urban designs connect
democratic planning
to sustainability
principles

Sustainist cities are
"Bright Green"**:
ecologically con-
scious, low in use of
resources, rich in
public transport and
energy-efficient
h o u s i n g ,
neighborhood-
minded, and sustain-
able consumers.

VERTICAL
ORGANICS

*Randolph T. Hester, *Design for Ecological Democracy*, 2006.
**Alex Steffen, *World Changing: A User's Guide for the 21st Century*, 2006.

Cities based
on local participation,
attachment to place,
community networks,
and sustainable thinking.

Place matters.
In a sustainable,
place-centered,
globalized urban politics*,
the meaning of both the "local"
and the "global"
is re-cast.

*Saskia Sassen, *A Sociology of Globalization*, 2007

Turning the city into a "sitopia," a "food-place"* (from the
Greek sitos, food, and topos, place).

*Carolyn Steel, *Hungry City: How Food Shapes Our Lives*, 2008.

CITIES

THAT ARE LOOKED AT

AS IF THEY WERE

GARDENS

WITH

STEWARDSHIP

& SUSTAINABLE

VALUES

sustainist globalization

Sustainist globalization =
development that is sustainable:
socially, ecologically and economically.

To move beyond
an economic globalization
that is at war with nature
and the poor.

Building on the positive power of globalization:
global connectedness
and global responsibility

A redefined globalism:
from "corporate globalization"
to "democratic globalization."

a shift in focus from globalized economics TO LOCAL LIVELIHOODS means a change in cultural perspectives

Fairness
enlarges the livelihoods
of the world's poor and
limits the claims to
resources of the
world's rich.*

Ecological concerns
are not a contradiction of
the elimination of poverty;
rather, they are its
condition.

For the poor,
sustainist living
means subsistence
and shelter.

.

*Inspired by Wolfgang Sachs et al.,
Fairness in a Fragile World: The Johannesburg Agenda, 2002

IN SUSTAINIST
DEVELOPMENT
fairness
AND
equity
ARE
ecological
AND
economic
necessities

an ecological

globalization

that is

autopoetic*

BEING ABLE TO RECYCLE

AND CLEAN ITSELF UP

THROUGH SELF ORGANIZATION

*Vandana Shiva, *Soil Not Oil: Climate Change, Peak Oil, and Food Insecurity*, 2009.

GLOBAL

GOALS

ARE

CONNECTED

TO   LOCAL

INITIATIVES

sustainist inclusiveness

O & I

AND / AND

RATHER THAN

either / or

sustainist

inclusiveness

gives voice to

the other

&

the indigenous

RECYCLED

Those from the affluent industrialized world (including the Western, European-born, privileged, white male authors of this manifesto) cannot speak for the dis-enfranchised and the poor—but need to accept this and hear their voice.

We
acknowledge our own
limitations: no viewpoint
is all-encompassing and all
of us are trapped within
our own fields
of vision.

In the sustainist era,
a manifesto is an open invitation to others:
to contribute to defining and making the future.

It is a movement that excludes no one.
Indeed, we are moving towards a sustainist world that
will come to include everyone.

embracing the

philosophy of

sharing

borrowing

& *lending*

that is open

to everyone

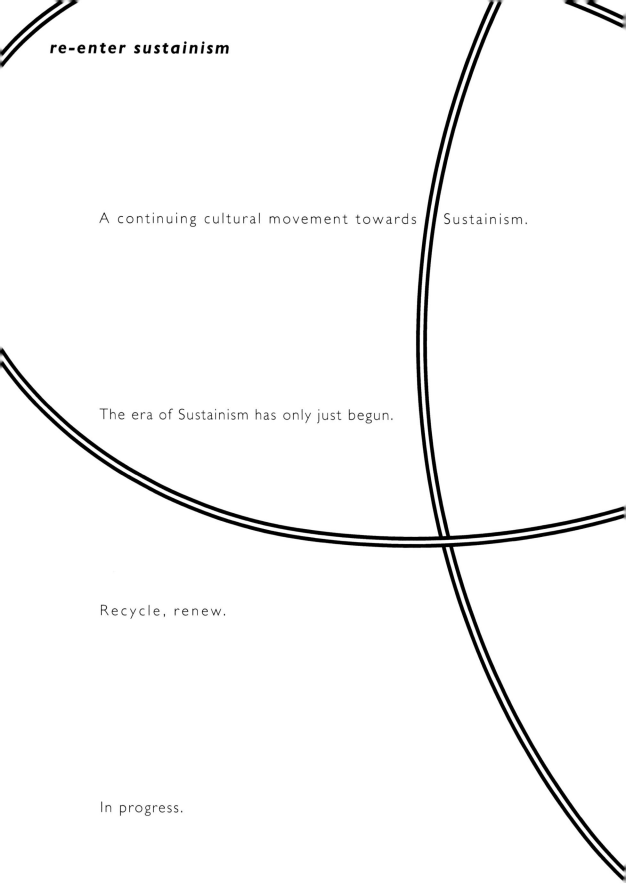

A continuing cultural movement towards Sustainism.

The era of Sustainism has only just begun.

Recycle, renew.

In progress.

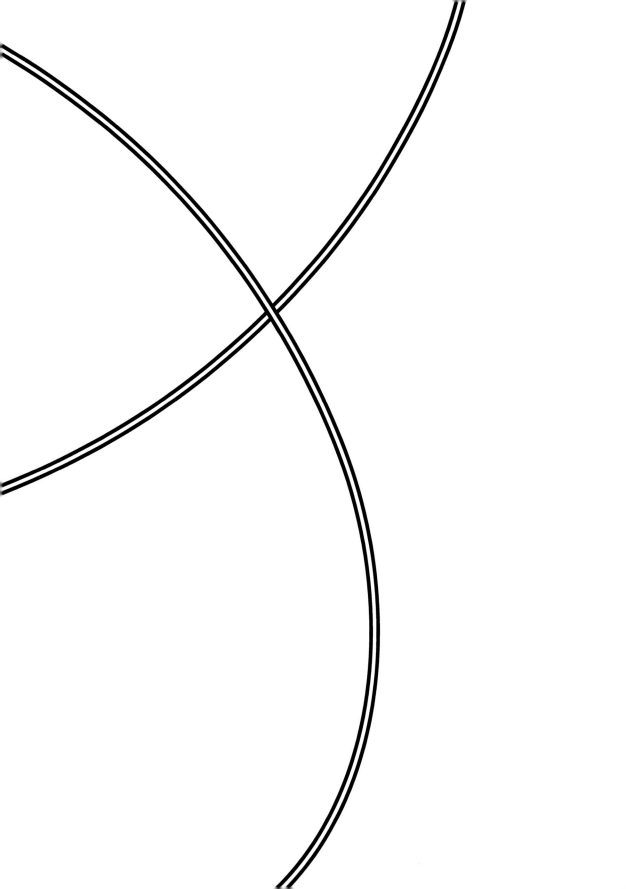

COMPOSTABLE

sustainism is
becoming the
state of the world.
it will soon come
to define our
lives and our
lifestyle.

WE
ARE
ALL
PART
OF
IT

the future is sustainist

sustainism is now

EPILOG

With this manifesto, we offer a vocabulary and a symbolic language for a new era.

A manifesto helps us see the beginning of the next possibility. This manifesto, unlike many others, is intentionally open-ended. It is a call to share and contribute to the ideas of Sustainism, in the Sustainist spirit of open-source culture. "We are what we share," as we propose in this book.

The trefoil knot symbolizes the interconnected nature of Sustainity, while other icons communicate essential Sustainist qualities such as "local" and "recyclable". These new icons are for practical use. We hope that others will find them inspiring and useful.

This manifesto is published under one of the "copyleft" licenses of the "Creative Commons". This means that our graphic symbols and statements can be used and distributed freely for non-commercial use (as long as we are credited in some way, and informed of the use). Commercial use is encouraged too, but requires our prior approval.

To chart the Sustainist revolution, we have borrowed freely (with full credit) from the leading thinkers and commentators of our age, from economists to ecologists, architects to activists, designers to media theorists and Sustainists avant la lettre such as Marshall McLuhan, E.F. Schumacher and Buckminster Fuller.

We are also happy to have been able to build on the ideas of the sustainability movement—the two million-plus non-profit organizations that collectively represent, as Paul Hawken has noted, "the largest movement in the world." We hope that this manifesto can contribute to the many local and global initiatives working to build a more equitable and more sustainable world.

This cultural manifesto has repositioned where we are, and re-imagines where we may be heading. Now we have to make the future. The Sustainist era has only just begun....

Share your thoughts: share@sustainism.com

www.sustainism.com

www.sustainism.com

Acknowledgements

In presenting Sustainism, we gratefully borrowed ideas from many.
Here we wish to acknowledge those who contributed directly to making the
manifesto what it is. We thank David Frankel for his textual and editorial
assistance, Wolfgang Sachs, Jon Else and Maarten Hajer for their insightful
comments and suggestions on the text, storyteller Joel ben Izzy, for his
enthusiastic help to sharpen the textual and visual narrative, and
Diana Sierra for her 3D design expertise.
Jesse Willenbring, our design assistant, deserves a special thanks for his
sustained effort —up until the final day— in shaping and reshaping this
book with us.
At Distributed Art Publishers we owe thanks to Sharon Helgason Gallagher,
D.A.P. executive director, for her encouraging support to our project,
and to Todd Bradway, D.A.P director of title acquisitions.
Some of the sustainist logos designed by Joost Elffers arose out of a
collaboration with Trefoil, a young Dutch "sustainable energy" company
set up by Benno Schwarz and Christiaan van Nispen.
We are grateful to those who have been supportive of our Sustainism
project and its further development, in particular Tim Brown, Janou Pakter,
Seth Goldstein, Stuart Rudick, Michela Bondardo, Aron Cramer, Annie Rattie,
Holton Rower, Susan Sgorbati, Will Hutchinson, Frederika Hunter,
Daniel Bruecher, William Ryman, Danny Adelson, Wellington Bowler and
Diana Krabbendam. Many others have provided inspiration, advice,
support and insight, among them Lindy Judge, Mikio Shinakawa,
Mania Lohrengel, Cori Olinghouse, Eduard Dekking, Toon Lauwen,
Niko Bruecher, Paul Mijksenaar, Frederick Doner, Siu Ling, Mark Mitton,
Sandy Rower, Flora Biddle Whitney, Molly Davies, Lily Cohen, Antje Landshoff,
Andreas Landshoff, Iwan Baan, Rob Ewaschuk, J.J. Spreij, Marc Schwarz,
Benno Schwarz, Louise van Santen, Jogi Panghaal, Mark Dowie, Jerry Mander,
Michael Pollan, Manuel Castells, Godfrey Reggio and Bill McKibben.
Two final personal acknowledgements. From Michiel— A special thank you to
Rody Luton, who accompanied this manifesto, inspired me, and in many ways
was involved in the creative process. And from Joost—
Thank you, Pat Steir, for casting your critical eye on our cultural statement,
and for showing me what it means to always give one's personal best.
Many people have inspired us over the years, and even though we cannot
pinpoint them specifically, they are present in this manifesto.

Michiel Schwarz, Joost Elffers.
Berkeley / New York, May 2010.

CONCEPT
Sustainism is the new modernism:
Joost Elffers, Michiel Schwarz

TEXT
Michiel Schwarz

DESIGN / LOGOS
Joost Elffers

DESIGN ASSISTANCE
Jesse Willenbring

Copyleft — the answer to Copyright. It is an addition to the restrictive "all rights reserved", creating a richer public domain. It is "some rights reserved", offering creators a best-of-both-world way to protect their work whilst encouraging certain uses for the sake of community, collaboration and sharing. The "copyleft" license we are using for this manifesto is one of the Creative Commons* licenses ("Attribution Non-Commercial No Derivatives"). This Creative Commons license allows redistribution and use of material from this work under certain conditions. It allows others to use and share our work as long as they credit us, but they cannot change the text or visuals in any way. Under this CC License, text and images cannot be used commercially or for financial benefits without authorization from the authors. When used or distributed non-commercially, our work should be credited as follows: Michiel Schwarz, Joost Elffers, *Sustainism is the New Modernism*, 2010.

www.sustainism.com

ABOUT MICHIEL SCHWARZ AND JOOST ELFFERS.

Michiel Schwarz is a Dutch independent cultural thinker, innovator and producer, currently working from Berkeley, California. Since completing his PhD in the sociology of technology at the University of London, he has worked as a cultural consultant and has advised public organizations in the Netherlands and other European countries. He has initiated a wide variety of projects exploring global issues, design, technology and progress. His publications include *The Technological Culture* (with Rein Jansma), *Divided We Stand* (with Michael Thompson) and *Speed: Visions of an Accelerated Age* (with Jeremy Millar).

Joost Elffers is a designer, cultural initiator and producer, who has inspired many creative book projects. He is in many ways a "symbol-maker." He is the creative producer of award-winning and innovative books, including *48 Laws of Power* (with Robert Greene), *Play with Your Food* (with Saxton Freymann) and *Tangram: The Ancient Chinese Shapes Game* (with Michael Schuyt). He lives and works in New York, having moved more than thirty years ago from his native Amsterdam, Netherlands.

d·a·p

D.A.P. / Distributed Art Publishers, Inc.
155 Sixth Avenue, 2nd Floor, New York, NY 10013.

 2010 by Michiel Schwarz, Joost Elffers.

Distributed in North America by D.A.P/Distributed Art Publishers, Inc., 155
Sixth Avenue, 2nd Floor, New York, New York, 11238.

Distributed outside of North America by Thames and Hudson Ltd., 181A High
Holborn, London WC1V 7QX, United Kingdom.

A CIP record for this book is available from the library of Congress.

ISBN 978-1-935202-22-6

Printed in China.